1950s
CHILDHOOD

Janet Shepherd & John Shepherd

Makes the Kiddies forget the Cake

Children love HOVIS because of its delicious flavour, as light dainty appearance and beautiful golden colour. So nourishing, too ! Grown-ups and tiny tots alike find in HOVIS the same generous source of nourishment which sustains strength and builds up bodily tissue after a strenuous day.

HōVIS
Trade Mark
Best Bakers Bake it

SHIRE PUBLICATIONS

Published in Great Britain in 2017 by Shire Publications
PO Box 883, Oxford, OX1 9PL, United Kingdom.
PO Box 3985, New York, NY 10185-3985, USA.
Email: shire@shirebooks.co.uk   www.shirebooks.co.uk

A CIP catalogue record for this book is available from the
British Library.

Shire Library no. 737.   ISBN-13: 978 0 74781 235 7

Janet Shepherd and John Shepherd have asserted their right
under the Copyright, Designs and Patents Act, 1988, to be
identified as the authors of this book.

Designed by Tony Trucott Designs, Sussex, UK
Typeset in Perpetua and Gill Sans.
Printed in China through World Print Ltd.

17 18 19   11 10 9 8 7 6 5 4

COVER IMAGE
Cover design by Peter Ashley. Front cover: illustration by
Ronald Lampitt from *The Map That Came to Life*, Oxford
University Press 1958; back cover detail: tin I-Spy badge
(author's collection).

TITLE PAGE IMAGE
A 1950s Hovis bread advertisement, aimed specifically
at families with young children, emphasised 'flavour
and nourishment'.

CONTENTS PAGE IMAGE
Reception class, Dronfield Infants' School, Derbyshire,
c. 1954. Several of the children are holding dictionaries
and ABC books.

ACKNOWLEDGEMENTS
We are most grateful to the following for providing
information and assistance: Mavis Battey; Bob Bateman;
Caroline Blake; Lesley and Ray Collier; Brenda and Grace
Corn; Sue and Colin Drummond; Mark Dunton; Sandra Lee;
Jessica Livingstone; Karen Livingstone; Francis Mallinson;
Nigel Neville; Christine and Ken Parry; Gill and Howard
Russell; Emma Shepherd; Louise Shepherd; Sandra and
Robert Shepherd; Gordon Teversham; DC Thomson; Debra
and Stephen Wade; Daniel Woodhouse; Cambridgeshire
Collection, Central Library, Cambridge; The Football
Association; Getty Archives; Robert Opie Collection;
Malcolm Barr-Hamilton, Tower Hamlets Archives.

Also, thank you to the many family and friends, especially in
Dry Drayton, who assisted or lent images that, for reasons
of space, could not be included. Thanks particularly to
Denise and Gary Glover and staff at the Black Horse public
house, Dry Drayton; all the staff at the Olive Tree Café in
Oakington; and to Sally and Simon Jones for their support
and encouragement.

Finally, a very special word of thanks to Les and Rose Waters
for expert technical assistance, advice and patience; and to our
commissioning editor, Ruth Sheppard at Shire Publications,
for her invaluable help and support.

Images are acknowledged as follows:
Advertising Archives, page 36; Bob Bateman, page 15
(top left); Mavis Battey, contents page; Butlins, page 47;
Cambridgeshire Collection, pages 12, 38, 46 (bottom) and 48
(top); Ray Collier, page 13; Cow & Gate, page 30 (bottom);
Evans Brothers, page 19 (bottom); Football Association, page
53 (top); Getty Images, pages 4, 8, 11, 26, 28, 41 (bottom),
49 (bottom), 50, 52 (bottom) and 53 (bottom); Ginn &
Co., page 19 (top); Hasbro, page 39 (top, Ludo, Draughts)
and 44 (top); G. J. Hayter, page 16 (top); HMSO, page 20
(bottom), 27, 33 (bottom); Honey Monster Foods, page 41
(top); Hoover, page 14 (top); Sandra Lee, page 30 (top);
Mirrorpix, page 46 (top), Nigel Neville, page 10; Robert
Opie Collection, page 16 (bottom right), 40 (bottom), 51
(bottom); Orion, page 51 (top); Ken Parry, page 24 (bottom),
33 (top); Random House, page 20 (top); Rank Hovis, title
page; Howard Russell, page 17 (bottom); Sampson Low, page
49 (top right); Janet Shepherd, pages 7, 15 (top right), 15
(bottom), 21 (bottom left), 22, 23, 24 (top), 39 (bottom),
40 (top), 45 (top), 48 (bottom); John Shepherd, pages
21 (bottom right), 25, 31 (top), 35, 42, 52 (top); Robert
Shepherd, page 21 (top); Gordon Teversham, page 17 (top);
D. C. Thomson, page 16 (bottom left); Tower Hamlets
Archives, page 45 (bottom); Weetabix Ltd, page 32.

Shire Publications is supporting the Woodland Trust, the UK's leading woodland conservation charity, by funding the dedication of trees.

CONTENTS

INTRODUCTION: FROM AUSTERITY TO AFFLUENCE

THE FORTUNATE GENERATION born after the Second World War, between 1946 and 1960, are now often identified as the 'baby-boomers', because birth rates soared as men returned from the armed forces to civilian life (a similar phenomenon had previously occurred after the First World War, with a hike in the birth rate that reached a peak in 1920). This generation, which is reaching retirement age in the second decade of the twenty-first century, is a feature of most western democracies and comprised about a quarter of the British population in 2013. Its best-known members include the pop stars Mick Jagger, Rod Stewart and Elton John, the politicians Edwina Currie, Tony Blair and Gordon Brown, the actress Maureen Lipman, the journalists Jon Snow, Melanie Phillips and Bel Mooney, and many other household names.

This book explores the lives of this generation of children, who constituted a massive rise in the United Kingdom population, and who grew up during some of the most interesting years in post-war Britain – the 1950s. It examines their health, homes, schooling, consumer habits and leisure pursuits as the decade progressed.

The 1950s, between the wartime 1940s and the permissive 1960s, was a time of change as well as some continuity. Early post-war austerity gradually turned into the affluence of the decade's later years, based on full employment, welfare state services and relative prosperity as mass consumer goods became increasingly available. By 1957 the mood of the nation was captured in Harold Macmillan's words: 'Most of our people have never had it so good.'

Demographic forecasts in the 1930s had visualised Britain moving towards a static, or even declining, population. However, after the advent of the Second World War, there was a sudden surge in the birth rate, and these predictions proved inaccurate.

The first boost occurred after soldiers returned on leave in 1942–3, followed by another increase at the end of the war, with births rising to a peak

Opposite:
'Cockneys' Own Party', Morpeth Street, in London's East End, held to celebrate the Coronation of Elizabeth II, 1953.

of over a million per annum by 1947. Other factors contributing to a post-war 'baby boom' included the extra allowances for soldiers with families, women's increased ability to support children financially due to increased wartime employment, and the opening of more pre-school nurseries.

The 1950s' baby-boomers have been depicted as 'uniquely healthier and wealthier', and more privileged than earlier or later generations. During more recent difficult economic times, they often feature as the subject of public debate over, for example, the provision of state pensions. This was the first 'National Health Service generation', nurtured from birth with a 'welfare state' providing free orange juice, milk and cod-liver oil to safeguard their health. At the start of the 1950s it was still a post-war world, with rationing and queues for basic food. Sugar, butter, cheese, margarine, cooking fat, bacon and tea were all still rationed. A final item, meat, did not come off ration until 4 July 1954. Memories of these years included home-made dresses, the lack of refrigerators, cold rooms and smelly paraffin heaters.

The broadcaster and writer Melvyn Bragg, eleven in 1950, thought 'respectability and aspiration' underpinned the decade. Traditional family values dominated: 'male breadwinners', full-time 'stay at home' married housewives, and '2.4 children'. In 1952 the psychoanalyst John Bowlby wrote a *News Chronicle* article titled, 'The mother who stays at home gives her children a better chance'. Francis Beckett, commenting on the early 1950s, wrote: 'it was illegal to buy *Lady Chatterley's Lover*, to get an abortion, to have a homosexual relationship, or stage a play without first obtaining permission from the Lord Chamberlain.'

However, such was the relief after the war years that the nation was very ready to celebrate events such as the 1951 Festival of Britain and the 1953 ascent of Mount Everest. Most notably, people came out onto the streets in their thousands for the coronation of Elizabeth II. Even more watched the event on the new medium of television. Television, perhaps more than anything else, revolutionised home life in the late 1950s, bringing recreation and entertainment into people's living rooms.

The post-war era placed a high importance on child welfare. Children were the future; it was 'to them the new welfare state was devoted'. The critical importance of the family as the 'indispensable framework' for a child's development was also recognised. Schooling for most was dominated by the Eleven Plus exam. The term 'meritocracy' – coined by the sociologist Michael Young in 1958 to mean IQ (Intelligence Quotient) + Effort = Merit – was very relevant in a decade 'obsessed with test-scores and qualifications'.

Americanisation gradually crept into many aspects of British life. The concept of the 'teenager' was created as youngsters embraced the new

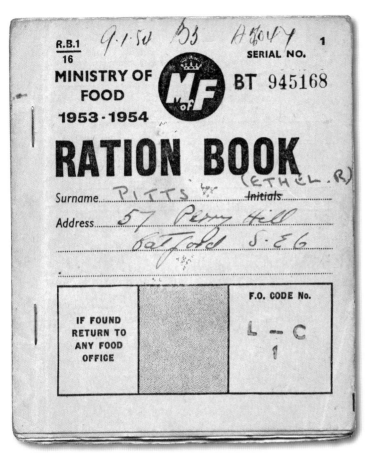

An adult's ration book for 1953–4, issued by the Ministry of Food, for 'eggs, fats, cheese, bacon, sugar, tea and sweets'.

culture from across the Atlantic, centred on 'teddy boys' and 'rock and roll', with its new stars such as Bill Haley and Elvis Presley.

By the later 1950s, with full employment and comprehensive welfare provision, working-class living standards steadily rose. The middle classes increasingly monopolised suburbia and, although the aristocracy had suffered financially, they still owned 50 per cent of the land. Although class divisions remained very evident, alongside growing racial tensions, life for most people began to improve as the decade progressed. Average weekly earnings rose by 34 per cent between 1955 and 1960, while most consumer items fell in price. The mantra 'Buy, buy, buy' at the end of the decade heralded the start of a burgeoning consumer age, and in the fast-developing world of popular music a baby-boomer group, the Beatles, was about to make its mark.

FAMILY LIFE

On winter mornings, I would reluctantly push my feet out of bed on to the cold linoleum floor, gingerly rub a circle in the lacy ice patterns that had formed inside the window pane, and peer out. Then, I would dress as fast as possible and hurtle downstairs to the only warm place – the kitchen.

FOR MANY CHILDREN, growing up in the 1950s meant living in a nuclear family, with two married parents and one or two siblings, where fathers went out to work and mothers were at home. This was certainly the conventional family unit, regularly portrayed in newspapers and magazines, on radio and, later, the new medium of television.

The 1950s have been described as a 'buttoned-down, conformist' decade, with marriage the general expectation and norm. Marriage legitimised sex, with alternative lifestyles viewed as unacceptable. As Frank Sinatra's 1955 hit song put it:

> Love and marriage, love and marriage,
> Go together like a horse and carriage.
> Dad was told by Mother,
> You can't have one without the other.

Divorce was rare and difficult to obtain, the only grounds being proven infidelity. By the end of the 1950s only one in five hundred marriages ended in divorce. Pejorative attitudes prevailed. The Christian-based Mothers' Union did not admit divorced or separated mothers. Children of divorced parents often felt stigmatised; one girl whose parents separated when she was twelve was advised by her grammar school head teacher to 'just get on with it'.

The central figure in most 1950s homes was the woman, as wife and mother. Although many women had worked on the 'home front' during the war, afterwards they were urged to return to domesticity. For those

Opposite:
Children playing
outside a house
in Royal Crescent,
Bath, c. 1955.

9

in paid work, gender influences, both at home and at school, meant that women were more likely to become secretaries, bank clerks, typists, hairdressers, nurses or teachers rather than engineers or scientists, seen as men's occupations.

Following the end of the war, housing became an urgent priority. One third of British homes had been affected by heavy bombing. Despite the initial post-war austerity experienced by all, there were distinct housing differences for children growing up in the 1950s. Many 1950s children, particularly in the London region, remember being moved out of the city centre into better housing in the suburbs. *Family and Kinship in East London* (Young and Willmott, 1957) was a landmark study of working-class families relocated in the 1950s from Bethnal Green to a new estate in Essex. The close-knit community feeling that had previously existed was difficult to maintain.

Huge council building programmes provided new flats, terraced and semi-detached houses, and prefabricated buildings ('prefabs'), intended as an economical short-term solution, but which often lasted for years. Large housing estates, such as Woodberry Down in north London, built by the London County Council in the immediate post-war years, provided relief from the capital's slums. The estate included rented flats with indoor bathrooms and toilets, new schools and a parade of twelve shops. Parts of the council estate afforded views, but no public access, to the two large Stoke Newington reservoirs. Such developments were hailed as the 'estates

The Neville family from Cambridge sit for a family portrait, c. 1950.

of the future' (*Daily Star*, 1949). Yet one boy whose family was rehoused at Woodberry Down in 1951 from the bomb sites of Islington remembers few modern amenities. In reality, home life meant cramped, damp accommodation, no central heating and a dirty coal bunker in the tiny kitchen.

Illustrations in the children's book *Peepo!* (Janet and Allan Ahlberg, 1981) also evoke an early 1950s' working-class childhood – a wartime gas mask still hangs on the brass bedhead, Mum wears an apron, there is an outside toilet, and the baby is washed in a tin bath in front of the coal fire.

Private housing was in demand as middle-class families increasingly sought homes with gardens for children to have space and fresh air. Some moved into accommodation in recently created 'new towns', such as Harlow and Stevenage.

The Evans family having tea in the new town of Harlow, Essex, 1958.

Population movements played an important part in shaping lives and destinies in Britain in the 1950s. From the late 1940s into the 1960s over 700,000 Britons emigrated to various countries in the British Empire and Commonwealth, most notably through the assisted '£10 passage' scheme to Australia. However, in 1987 a Nottingham social worker, Margaret Humphreys, uncovered the scandalous forcible deportation of British children in care in the post-war period. Churches and charitable organisations sent them to Commonwealth countries, especially Australia. Her book *Empty Cradles* (1994) exposed how many of the children lost their identities and many were erroneously told their parents were dead.

Historically, Irish, Jewish, Huguenot and other immigrants had made a significant contribution to the diversity of British life and culture. In 1948 the arrival of the troopship *ImperialWindrush*, bringing 492 official immigrants across the Atlantic, was a landmark in the development of multicultural Britain. In the 1950s many migrants, mainly from Ireland and the Caribbean, were recruited by successive British governments to work in hospitals, transport and other essential services. By 1955 immigrants from the 'New Commonwealth' numbered around 27,500 *per annum*, playing an important role in the upturn of the British economy.

However, 'black immigration' became a social and political issue. Often forced to settle in already overcrowded inner-city areas, the new families faced intense racism, most notably the violent Notting Hill riots in the summer of 1958, exacerbated by far-right groups pledged to 'keep Britain white'. Sadly, being subjected to racist taunts became a norm for many immigrant children. The Notting Hill Carnival, later the 'largest street fair

Children regularly played in the street in the 1950s, there being less traffic than now, and fewer recreational areas. This is Gothic Street, Cambridge.

in Europe', evolved from 1959 as a positive response to deteriorating race relations in west London.

Wherever they lived, children regularly played outside, often with the streets as their playground. John remembers playing on a wartime bomb site in Baxter Road, Islington. In an enterprising project, a neighbour, Mrs Whittlebury, paid local children 6d, and bottles of lemonade, to clear a path across the rubble so that she could reach the local pub more quickly.

At the start of the decade daily shopping and cooking from scratch were the norm; there were no 'ready meals'. Before refrigerators, small cold rooms – larders – were used to keep food cool. Milk bottles stood in bowls of cold water but if the milk curdled it could be used to make scones, so as not to waste any. If bacon became mouldy, the mould would be washed off before cooking it.

Reins were commonly used to restrain young children in the 1950s. Three-year-old Ray Collier stands in Rheidol Terrace, Islington, c. 1955. The 'bag laundry', on the corner opposite the child's tricycle, was demolished when Islington Green School was built in the 1960s.

After more than a decade of rationing, Britain was a 'plain food' nation with a 'meat, potato and well-boiled cabbage culture'. The 1950s' diet was high in fat, and nearly every meal contained meat. Favourites were stew with dumplings, corned beef hash, Spam fritters, 'toad in the hole', offal, rabbit stew, tinned meats and beef dripping on toast, followed by steamed puddings, milk puddings or jelly and custard. The only fresh fruit and vegetables available were seasonal, with children frequently given the summer job of shelling peas from the pods, but fruit was bottled for the winter in Kilner jars, sealed with glass stoppers and metal clamps. Strawberries appeared for a few weeks during the summer and, during the austerity years, bananas were imported for children only. Few families ate out, and tea was still the national beverage. There was no coffee except for Camp coffee essence, which has been described as 'undrinkable'. Children drank diluted orange squash; fizzy drinks, apart from lemonade, were rare.

When rationing ended, food became more varied and plentiful, with a continuing increase in the consumption of meat. The 'new' food was chicken: formerly usually eaten only at Christmas and Easter, it could now be bought frozen, together with frozen vegetables, as more people acquired refrigerators.

Housework was physically demanding. Most children remember their mothers using mangles to squeeze out the family wash, still mostly done by hand. Later, in the improving economy, there was a transformation in the kitchen – hard-wearing Formica worktops, Kenwood mixers, non-stick pans, refrigerators and twin-tub washing machines. Plastic became the new sought-after material.

An advertisement for a Hoover cleaner in the Festival of Britain guide, 1951. Labour-saving equipment began to be advertised from the early 1950s but was not commonplace until later in the decade.

Progress in the Home

Hoover Limited take pride in the fact that their products are saving millions of housewives from hard, wearisome drudgery — not only in Britain but throughout the world. Wherever the name Hoover appears it is a guarantee of excellence.

THE WORLD-FAMOUS HOOVER CLEANER

The Hoover Cleaner, with its famous triple-action principle — " It beats . . . as it sweeps . . . as it cleans " — is undeniably the world's best cleaner — best in design, best in materials, best in quality of workmanship. There is a model suitable for every size and type of home.

THE MARVELLOUS HOOVER ELECTRIC WASHING MACHINE

The Hoover Electric Washing Machine has completely revolutionised the whole conception of washing-day in the home. It does the full weekly wash for a large family and yet is such a handy size—suitable for even the smallest kitchen.

VISIT THE HOOVER FACTORY
Visitors to the Festival of Britain are cordially invited to make a tour of the Hoover Factories at Perivale, Middlesex, or Merthyr Tydfil, South Wales, or Cambuslang, Scotland. Please write to, Hoover Limited, Perivale, or 'phone Perivale 3311 for more information.

HOOVER LIMITED

Factories at :
MIDDLESEX · MERTHYR TYDFIL · HIGH WYCOMBE · CAMBUSLANG, SCOTLAND

Meccano, made of metal in the 1950s, was the decade's biggest-selling construction toy.

In the days before television, children's evenings, especially in the winter, were spent playing with toys or reading. Alec would spend Saturday evenings at home in Cambridge. While his mother sewed or darned and his father had his one bath of the week, Alec listened to the radio and played with marbles or wooden bricks, while his older brother made Meccano models. Lego arrived in 1953; Playdoh in 1956.

Toys were mostly gender-based. In the post-war years guns were very popular with boys, as were tin soldiers, and model

tin cars made by Dinky, Corgi and Matchbox. Later, Matchbox's red London bus was a commercial success; by 1960 the firm was producing a million 'fit in your hand' toy cars each day. Girls often had toy farms with miniature metal animals and people. Teddy bears and dolls retained their popularity, while dolls' houses, often home-made in early austerity Britain, continued to have great appeal. Noah's Ark appeared in different guises, often in wooden models and jigsaws.

Above left: Advertisement for Dinky Toys. Dinky's models were so authentic that its yellow Weetabix lorry was ordered in bulk by Weetabix as a promotional giveaway.

The weekly comic was an important part of growing up and there was a large choice, including *Dandy*, *Beezer*, *Topper*, *Wizard*, *Rover* and *Hotspur*, but by far the most popular was *Beano*. For older boys there was *Eagle*, with its adventurous hero, Dan Dare. Its counterpart, *Girl*, full of middle-class heroines, was avidly read by girls, as were *School Friend* and *Girls' Crystal*. One young reader recalled: 'My heart would miss a beat when *School Friend* arrived

Above right: A home-made dolls' house built from orange boxes by a little girl's father, early 1950s. Discarded orange boxes were also often used to make go-carts and, at the height of austerity, even basic furniture such as bookshelves.

Left: Treasured celluloid dolls from *c.* 1955.

through the front door, especially if "The Silent Three" [masked girls solving crimes] were on the front page in full colour.'

Annuals continued to amuse and delight, as also did Penguin's colourful non-fiction 'Picture Puffins' and Puffin Story Books — a series of reprinted classics and modern stories. Books published in the 1950s that won awards and remained popular throughout the twentieth century and beyond included *The Borrowers* (Mary Norton, 1952), the 'Narnia' books (C. S. Lewis, 1949–56) and *Tom's Midnight Garden* (Philippa Pearce, 1958).

Above: A Noah's Ark jigsaw puzzle, made of wood. Wooden jigsaws, sometimes very intricate with many pieces, were common in the 1950s.

By 1949 clothes were no longer rationed, but remained very utilitarian for several years. With only a limited choice in the shops, children wore smaller versions of what the adults were wearing.

Most housewives made and mended the family's clothes. John Woodhouse recalls his mother buying leather in Chapel Street market, Islington, to mend his shoes: 'Mum was expert in choosing the best pieces of leather, very even in thickness, but pliable.'

Right: The *Beano* comic for 7 July 1956, costing '2d each Thursday'. The *Beano*'s most famous character, Dennis the Menace, first appeared in 1951.

Far right: The *Rupert Annual* continued to be very successful throughout the 1950s.

Until they started secondary school, boys wore short trousers. Girls had knee-length dresses, or skirts worn with blouses and hand-knitted cardigans. One exception to girls' plain clothes was the smocked party dress, with a wide waist band tied in a bow at the back. Most children had only one pair of shoes, 'lace-ups', suitable for

school. For many families, economy was essential. A 1955 Clydella advertisement featured a girl's short-sleeved blouse ('How it wears and washes!'). Older girls favoured belted 'shirt-waister' dresses, worn over stiffly starched frilly 'cancan' petticoats that made the dresses flare out in a circle – perfect for dancing rock and roll in the latest 'slip-on' shoes, but the essential daily starching took a lot of time and starch.

The term 'teenager' began to appear in the 1950s, as youngsters became heavily influenced by American trends, especially after such films as *Blackboard Jungle* and *Rebel without a Cause*, whose leading actor, James Dean, became a cult icon after his early death in a 1955 car crash. Michelle Hanson was impressed by airmen from a local US base, with their 'crew cuts, bobby socks and blue jeans'. From the mid-1950s a new, mainly working-class, youth sub-culture appeared: the 'teddy boys', associated with rock and roll music and Elvis Presley – 'the King'. With their distinctive Edwardian revival image – velvet collars, drainpipe trousers and quiff haircuts – teddy boys were portrayed in the media as violently anti-establishment and unnerved the middle classes. Many youngsters, teddy boys or otherwise, were regarded as rebellious, disrespectful delinquents, and this clash between teenagers and their parents became known as the 'generation gap'.

Teenager Howard Russell was extremely proud of his 'up to the minute' Kodak Junior II camera, purchased in July 1958.

SCHOOLDAYS

The year was 1955. We stood in silent lines at the back of the school hall staring in trepidation at our headmaster, Mr Lord. Slowly he called out the names. I heard mine, then waited to hear my friend Richard's. It didn't come. We, the chosen ones, walked to the front to be clapped by those who weren't called. We had 'passed' the scholarship, they had not.

EDUCATION became a priority in post-war Britain. The 1944 'Butler' Education Act, and the similar Education (Scotland) Act, 1945, heralded a brave new world of secondary education for all, with a national distinction at eleven between primary and secondary sectors. For the first time universal free secondary education would be provided for all children in England and Wales up to eighteen, including part-time provision for sixteen-to eighteen-year-olds in new county colleges. From 1947 the school-leaving age rose from fourteen to fifteen.

The 1944 Act did not stipulate any one system of secondary education, recommending instead a range of provision suitable for 'different abilities and aptitudes'. In practice, the secondary system run by local education authorities (LEAs) after the war was a diverse regional patchwork, comprising grammar, modern, technical, a few 'central' and, gradually, a number of comprehensive schools. The proposed county colleges were never built. As there were few technical or central schools providing vocational education (except in London), what largely emerged by the 1950s was a bipartite system of grammar and modern schools with very different curricula. While, in the immediate post-war years, Anglesey was the first LEA with a fully comprehensive system, most comprehensives did not arrive until the 1960s.

Prevailing educational thought firmly favoured testing to determine which branch of secondary schooling each child was most suited to. The 'Eleven Plus' examination (or 'scholarship'), determined a child's educational future with tests in mathematics, English language and verbal reasoning (or 'intelligence'), all usually conducted on one day in the final year of primary school. Although the 1944 Education Act had envisaged equality, or 'parity of esteem', between the different secondary schools, popular misconceptions developed that those who secured a grammar school place had 'passed' the Eleven Plus, whereas those who went to 'secondary moderns' had 'failed'. Even many teachers, as well as parents, viewed the Eleven Plus as a 'pass/fail' examination.

The booming birth rate and the raising of the school-leaving age (ROSLA) meant that by September 1948 there were thousands of primary and secondary age children urgently needing both new teachers and accommodation. A twelve-month Emergency Training Scheme (ETS) for teachers began in 1945. Many recruits were returning servicemen, selected more for personality than academic qualifications. By 1951 35,000 ETS teachers were employed, making 'a substantial contribution'. A record number of 928 new primary schools were built between 1945 and 1950. With a severe shortage of labour and materials, one solution was prefabricated buildings. HORSA ('Hutting Operation for ROSLA') began, and temporary huts, with concrete floors, metal windows and asbestos roofs, appeared in school playgrounds all over Britain.

By the early 1950s most primary age children, from five to eleven, attended all-ability, co-educational, local authority schools. Approximately a third of schools were church-run; their future was secured after the 1944 Act incorporated existing church schools into the state system.

With the influx of baby-boomers, some classes were very large. There were sixty reception-class children at St Paul's Church of England Primary School, Bournemouth, in the early to mid-1950s. Inevitably 'whole-class teaching', inherited from Victorian elementary schools, remained the easiest way to maintain order. While nursery-age children might have a post-lunch nap on fold-up camp beds, many five-year-olds in large classes were seated in rows for much of the day. Slates and chalk were still in use in infant classes in the early 1950s.

The primary curriculum emphasised the '3Rs' (reading, writing and arithmetic), and much was still learned by rote. Many schools used the phonics-based 'Beacon' scheme to teach reading but by the later 1950s

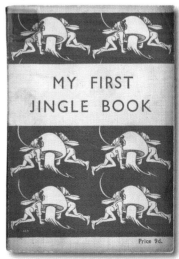

The *Beacon Supplementary Readers Book Four* and *My First Jingle Book* were both based on a phonics approach to reading, whereby children learn to sound out letters and words.

Singing Together, a booklet to accompany BBC broadcasts to schools, autumn term 1958. It included the song 'Cockles and Mussels', the 'Sussex Carol' and a synopsis of Amahl and the Night Visitors.

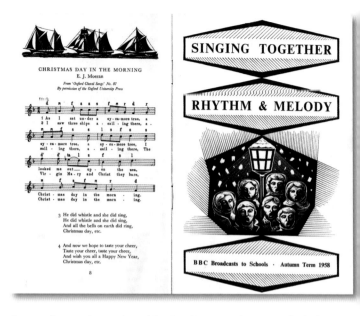

this was frequently supplanted by Ginn's *Janet and John*, in which the main characters were portrayed as 'average middle-class English children'.

Little science was taught, but there was nearly always a nature table, with 'interesting bits' found on occasional 'nature walks'. Some fortunate children listened to BBC Schools radio programmes, such as *Singing Together*, when two or three classes would combine to sing traditional songs.

Under the 1944 Act daily non-denominational assemblies were compulsory. Most 1950s' children remember singing hymns, including 'All Things Bright and Beautiful' with its class-bound, and later banned, verse:

The rich man in his castle,
The poor man at his gate,
God made them high and lowly
And ordered their estate...

In general, pupils knew who was 'bright' and who was not, just as

Writing with a dip pen was an acquired skill. Too much ink resulted in blobs, too little and scratches appeared. Crossed nibs, when one side of the nib stuck on top of the other, were a frequent hazard.

everyone knew who was 'poor' and receiving free school meals. Primary children were often seated in order of test results, with the 'top child' perhaps at the front on the left, and the 'bottom child' at the back on the right. Desks had flip-up lids and inkwells holding ink for 'dip-pens', small wooden holders with removable metal nibs. Michelle Hanson recalled that

Mr Turner's class at Woodberry Down Primary School, 20 July 1955.

Pupils at many secondary schools compiled school magazines at the end of the educational year, with contributions from most year groups: *Hendon County Grammar School Magazine*, July 1959; *The Highburian*, Highbury Grammar School, July 1954.

'new technology meant a lever fountain pen', possibly kept in an 'up to the minute' plastic roll-top pencil case.

Black pot-bellied wood-burning stoves were often used to heat classrooms. Nearby, crates of milk in one-third of a pint (120 ml) glass bottles with silver tops would stand warming up, ready for drinking at morning break. Milk was still freely available at secondary level and many schools also had tuck shops selling penny iced buns or jam doughnuts at break time.

Inside lavatories were rare; there would just be separate outside blocks ('that always smelt') for girls and boys, built of shiny orange bricks. School dinners were not always available on site. Children at St Paul's School walked in crocodile formation each lunchtime to Alma Road School, where 'Waste not, want not' was the dictum. In many primary schools girls spent playtimes with skipping ropes, boys with marbles or cigarette cards.

Hendon County Grammar School's choir, with awards won in 1957.

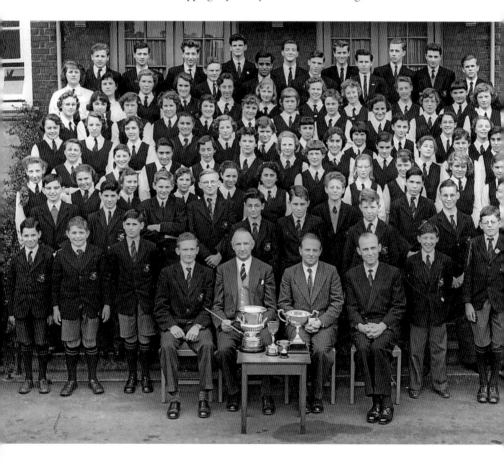

At all levels, schooling was full of rules and strict discipline. Brunswick Infants' School in Cambridge was divided into a girls' and a boys' school on the same site, and the playground was 'split with a white line that must never be crossed'. Parents were generally unwelcome in school and even very young children had to say goodbye at the school gate. Pupils were often 'made an example of' to deter others. Raymond had to go round all the classes in his Norwich school with a note pinned to his jumper stating, 'I must not be late or come to school with dirty hands'. Corporal punishment was common; in a 1952 national poll, 89 per cent of teachers voted to retain it. Boys were frequently caned on the backside, girls hit on the hand or knuckles with a ruler. Some teachers regularly threw chalk or even board rubbers at inattentive children. At secondary level, 'lines' – copying the same sentence repeatedly in best handwriting – were frequently given, as were also detentions, when recalcitrant children were kept at school after home time.

By the time children reached the top end of the primary school, the Eleven Plus examination dominated their education. 'Teaching to the test' was common everywhere, with pupils repeatedly practising exam papers in order to score as many marks as possible. In some cases children were privately coached, or promised a new bicycle, if they 'passed' the Eleven Plus. Many children were scarred by the experience. Cliff Richard stated that 'failing' the Eleven Plus had ruined his 'confidence in any kind of written examination'. Greg Dyke recalled that when his brother 'failed' it was viewed as a family tragedy.

The fourth form at Hendon County Grammar School, July 1956.

DETAILED REPORT

The Grades used are A, B, C, D. In a representative group of eight pupils there will be approximately one A, three B's, three C's and one D.

Subject	Grade	Remarks	Initials of Teacher
Scripture	A	Good work	LS
Handwriting	B		OE
Speech ..	A		OE
English Language ..	A.	Excellent.	OE
English Literature ..			
History ..	B+ B.	Very good class work.	JWE
Geography ..			
French ..	B—	Improved.	D
German ..			
Latin	3	Good effort + progress	JWH
Arithmetic ..			
Algebra ..	B	Janet has now become more	JWH
Geometry ..		confident & improved considerably.	
Advanced Maths. ..			
Chemistry ..	C-	Hampered by absence at the beginning of term	JS
Physics ..	B	Good	AoE
Biology ..	B	Satisfactory.	BBO
Art	B+	Good.	WR
Geometrical Drawing			
Manual Instruction ..			
Domestic Science ..			

A typical 'detailed' school report from 1955. Far from being detailed, reports often contained just minimal comments by the teacher and an alphabetical grade for each subject.

Smartly dressed science sixth-formers at Manchester Grammar School, 1956.

As the 1950s progressed, grammar schools were in their heyday in an education system that starkly perpetuated the class system. Most grammar school pupils were middle-class, while the majority attending secondary moderns were working-class. Working-class children who secured a grammar school place might find themselves in an incomprehensible middle-class world.

Grammar schools often operated further rigorous internal 'streaming'. The journalist Joan Bakewell's description of Stockport High School for Girls, where the A classes learned Latin and the B classes domestic science, was repeated across the country. In 1958 at Hendon County School, a co-educational grammar school in north London, a twelve-year-old child in the Latin stream was advised by the headmaster 'not to mix with the domestic science girls'.

General Certificate of Education (GCE) Ordinary (O) and Advanced (A) level examinations began in 1951. The new exams (O levels at sixteen, A levels at eighteen) were designed for the top 25 per cent. The pass standard was considerably higher than the old School and Higher School Certificates, making the chance of a child passing significantly less. In 1952

BURY SCHOOL DRAMATIC SOCIETY
PRESENTS
MAJOR BARBARA
By GEORGE BERNARD SHAW
n Wednesday December 14th, 1955
IN THE SCHOOL HALL
Commencing 7.30.p.m.   Doors open 7.00.p.m.
TICKET 3/-   ROW F NO. 9

the *Daily Mirror* commented on the first year's results: 'In every general subject, such as English or Maths, nearly half the candidates failed to secure a pass.' Results gradually improved but, throughout the decade, only the top 3–4 per cent went on to university.

Many grammar schools were single-sex. Boys and girls from neighbouring schools were often actively discouraged from meeting. At school dances, always ballroom and strictly monitored by staff, the opposite sex might be invited. Girls and boys would sit facing each other across the school hall. Only the bravest boys summoned up the courage to cross the divide and ask a girl to dance. School drama productions in single-sex schools presented problems. At Highbury School, north London, and in many other boys-only schools, the girls' parts were played by boys.

Secondary school uniform was generally mandatory, enforced by watchful staff. Caps for boys, and berets or hats for girls, had to be worn to and from school. Children were inventive, however: girls' berets were often folded in half, and fixed to the head with kirby grips; with the hair back-combed over it, the beret all but disappeared. The popular mid-1950s' starched petticoats

The single-sex Highbury Grammar School put on a production of George Bernard Shaw's *Major Barbara* in 1955, where the female roles were played by boys.

Secondary modern schools taught a practical curriculum. A teacher at Ryder Brow Secondary School, Manchester, demonstrates how to thread a sewing machine, 4 February 1956.

were banned at Hendon County School as they 'pushed gymslip skirts almost horizontal to the waist'.

During the 1950s approximately three-quarters of all secondary age children were educated in secondary modern schools with a curriculum 'free from the rigours of exams'. While grammar schools focused on 'learning for its own sake', secondary moderns educated children about 'concrete things [rather] than ideas'.

Although a few secondary modern children sat GCEs, the majority left school at fifteen with no qualifications and restricted job opportunities. Expectations, from both schools and parents, were frequently low. One baby-boomer recalled:

> Having 'failed' my Eleven Plus, I was consigned, along with most of my friends, to a secondary modern in King's Cross. After two years, alongside our schoolwork, we could choose apprenticeships in carpentry, plumbing, bricklaying, or signwriting. The latter appealed to me, but my father steered me towards 'a real job like bricklaying'.

Some secondary moderns, however, were progressive and gradually provided a wider curriculum to give their pupils a broader range of scientific and cultural knowledge, as well as the opportunity to take examinations. The forward-looking Crowther Report (1959), commenting on the education of children aged fifteen to eighteen, stated that secondary modern education often resulted in 'a waste of talent'. Its recommendation to increase the school-leaving age to sixteen was not, however, implemented until 1972.

By the later 1950s it was clear that the grammar/secondary-modern model was being increasingly superseded by single 'all-ability' comprehensive schools, particularly popular in large cities such as London and Manchester, and some rural areas. In 1957 there were thirty-two comprehensives, with twenty-one on the way, all taking children across the full ability range. Despite this development, the Ministry of Education still advocated the 1944 model of education. A 1958 government White Paper, *Secondary Education for All, A New Drive* proposed retaining grammar schools and just extending the courses on offer in secondary modern schools.

Britain's first purpose-built comprehensive, Kidbrooke School in south London, opened in 1954 for two thousand girls and became the prototype for the changing face of education. However, it was insufficiently resourced, and its impact was diminished by its huge size and by the fact that grammar schools were permitted to exist alongside the new school, thus 'creaming off' many of the brighter pupils. This often remained a controversial political issue in secondary education, even with the growth of more comprehensives in the 1960s and 1970s. However, for many in 2013, the 1950s still represent a golden age of the British grammar school.

Secondary modern pupils set up a weather station and learn to measure rainfall, *c.* 1950s.

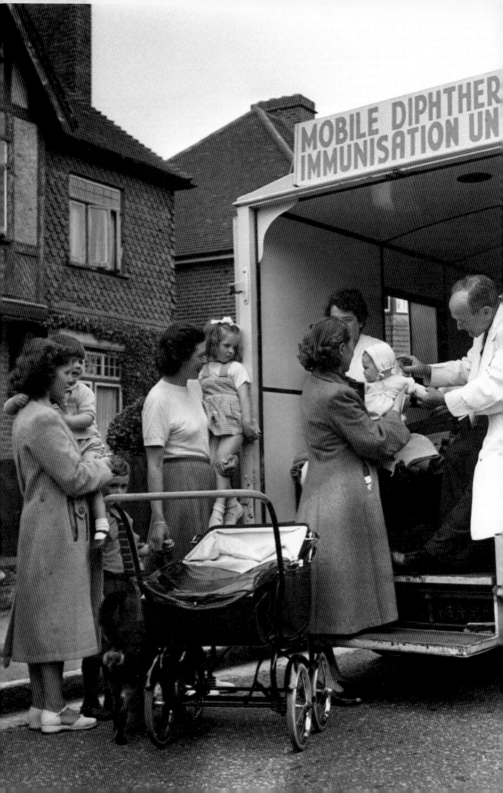

HEALTH

When I was nine I contracted polio. I spent several weeks in a ward on my own ... no visitors until I was out of danger and then my Mum could only stand outside an open window to talk to me. No touching. I didn't see my Dad or little brother all the time I was in hospital. Polio affected my joints, leaving me with very weak ankles and wrists. But I was lucky. Another girl my age died.

O N 5 July 1948 Labour's Health Minister, Aneurin Bevan, opened the Park Hospital in Manchester, and Britain's National Health Service (NHS) began. Children born after 1948 were the first to benefit from a health service incorporating 'hospitals, nurses, pharmacists, opticians and dentists' within a single organisation. For the first time comprehensive medical care was provided 'free at the point of delivery', financed entirely from taxation. In a 1956 survey 90 per cent of patients approved of the new service.

The first purpose-built 'health centre for the future' was the John Scott Medical Centre on Woodberry Down Council Estate, Hackney – 'a bright new building incorporating all the latest ideas in social medicine' – which opened in a blaze of national publicity in 1952. In addition to adult care, the centre specialised in children's health, offering ante-natal services, child welfare, school and dental health, all under one roof. Before long, costs proved far higher than had been anticipated, and the unprecedented demand for NHS treatment prohibited the creation of any more purpose-built centres. Charges began to be introduced for prescriptions, spectacles and dental treatment, thus eroding the concept of completely free treatment. Children's services, however, remained exempt.

One of the NHS's aims was actively to promote good health, not just to provide treatment. Much attention was given to improving children's physical welfare and providing better experiences for mothers and babies during pregnancy and childbirth. For the first time babies in the womb

Opposite:
The NHS urged parents to get their children immunised against certain deadly diseases. In Portsmouth in 1951 mothers queued at a mobile van for their children to receive diphtheria immunisation.

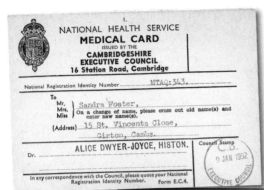

were monitored by ultrasound. Induction became available, also epidurals for difficult births. In addition to school milk, the new NHS also provided subsidised orange juice, malt, and regular doses of cod-liver oil (not always enjoyed) for young children. Powdered National Dried Milk for babies, fortified with vitamin D, continued to be available for many years. Belief in the benefits of

Each NHS patient was issued with a medical card and an individual identity number.

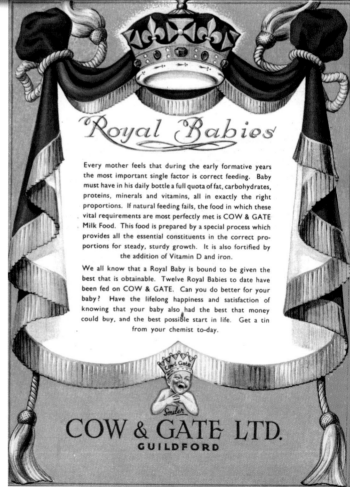

In the 1951 Festival of Britain guide, a Cow & Gate advertisement proudly stated that 'twelve royal babies to date have been fed on Cow & Gate' baby milk formula.

fresh air meant that most babies slept outside during daytime hours, in gardens or outside the front door, often in large Silver Cross prams.

Some expectant mothers pressed for less, not more, intervention, and in 1956 the National Childbirth Association (later Trust) was founded, promoting natural, drug-free childbirth. Hugely successful, it received charitable status in 1961. Additionally, the National Child Development Study began to be collated from the late 1950s, when medical data was taken from a random sample of almost 17,500 babies born in one week in 1958.

The vast majority of 1950s babies were born in wedlock. Rates of illegitimacy were low and to become an unmarried mother was frequently a disaster. The shame of single motherhood stigmatised both mother and child. Abortion was illegal and, even if a 'back-street' abortionist could be found, the procedure was expensive and dangerous, as was shown in the award-winning 2004 film *Vera Drake*, set in London in 1950. Most unmarried pregnant girls had no option but to give their babies up for adoption, creating for many a psychological trauma they carried for the rest of their lives.

Post-war children were the first to receive free school dental checks. In the days before fluoride, many had several fillings before they were ten. Visits to the dentist could be painful and traumatic. Drills were often old, cumbersome and slow. Injections were rarely given for fillings. For extractions, gas was administered via a rubber face mask. Children spoke of the fear and the unpleasant smell of the mask, followed by bad dreams and sickness.

In an attempt to stop the early deterioration of children's eyesight, the NHS provided free spectacles, so popular that the allocated £2 million, intended to last nine months, ran out in the first six weeks. Children who wore free glasses were often teased for wearing 'NHS specs', as their basic round lenses created an owl-like appearance.

At the start of the decade rationing limited both the quality and the quantity of food, most notably in towns. Families who managed to grow their own vegetables had healthier options. The popular children's author Enid Blyton regularly listed what her characters liked to eat. In *Five on a Hike Together* (1951), the town children are in the countryside, delighted by 'home-made meat pie … home pickled cabbage, onions and beetroot'.

By 1954 more than 50 per cent of children received a hot midday meal at school, generally meat with two vegetables and a cooked dessert. At home many children were required to drink

Free National Health spectacles, worn by John Shepherd, c. 1952.

Austerity cooking led to ingenuity. This recipe uses rabbit instead of the more expensive chicken to make a 'mock chicken' casserole.

HOT LUNCH SAVOURIES
••••••••••••••••••••••••••••••••
MOCK CHICKEN CASSEROLE

Maggi Chicken flavoured Noodle Soupmix (one box only), 3 or 4 pieces of rabbit, ½ lemon.

Wash the rabbit and rub with lemon to whiten the flesh. Rinse with cold water. Cover with cold water, bring to the boil. Drain well.
Place the tablet of Soupmix in a casserole with the rabbit and one pint of boiling water. Cover, bake for 1½ hours in a moderate oven 375°F (mark 4). Add the Noodles, replace the lid and cook for a further ½ hour. Garnish with chopped parsley and serve with vegetables.

the nutritional water left over from boiling vegetables. Sick children were commonly given warm milk and Lucozade, regularly advertised in the 1950s as an 'aid to recovery' and the 'nice part about being ill'.

Boarding-school children often received a very restricted diet, even after the end of rationing. One pupil, Chris, recalled her boarding-school food in 1956: 'The school still rationed butter and marge, two ounces of each for a week in a dish, and three ounces of sugar in a honey jar, both with names written on zinc oxide tape stuck to the lid.'

In general, however, there was a concerted effort to ensure children received a healthy, nourishing diet. By the end of the decade both the quality and the quantity of food had greatly improved compared with the limited options of earlier years.

To ensure good health, daily physical exercise was considered essential for children's health and well-being. Her Majesty's Stationery Office (HMSO) produced two progressive books: *Moving and Growing* (1952) examined children's growth and physical development in great detail; *Planning the Programme* (1953) pioneered modern, innovative teaching methods, emphasising broader physical *education* (PE), rather than the old physical *training* (PT) still practised in more traditional schools.

Weetabix, the 'perfect family breakfast', c. 1950s.

A highlight for some primary-age children, especially in London, was a weekly swimming lesson at the local public baths. A few schools even managed to install their own pool. Parents at Underhill Junior School, Barnet, raised sufficient money for an outdoor pool. Twenty years later, another group of parents paid for the pool to be roofed. It was still in use in 2013.

In the days before central heating, thick warm clothing was considered essential for health, with many young children swaddled in layers of woollen clothes. This was still the era of the liberty bodice, a sleeveless thick undergarment worn by girls, in addition to a vest, with 'rubber buttons to stop them hurting the skin that took ages to do up'. One girl, Pamela, remembers being 'trussed up like a turkey' in 'vest, liberty bodice, blouse, pinafore dress, jumper and finally a raincoat'. Most schoolgirls wore warm voluminous thick knickers, navy, green or brown, often with a pocket for a handkerchief.

A very formal
indoor physical
training session
at Darlington
Grammar School,
c. 1952.

'Physical education
can help children
develop their full
powers,' stated
HMSO's 1952 book
Moving and Growing.

Girls did not wear trousers, so chapped knees were common in cold winters, and red marks appeared on legs, caused by the tight elastic bands used to stop long socks from slipping down.

Although the old childhood killer diseases were gradually disappearing, epidemics still occurred. In a 1956 polio epidemic a few thousand children between the ages of two and nine were vaccinated, but there was insufficient vaccine available for all. Furthermore, some parents, unsure about the vaccine's safety, refused to allow their children to be vaccinated. This resulted in three thousand people, mostly children, contracting the disease. Diphtheria vaccinations were available from the start of the decade, and by the mid-1950s polio and diphtheria vaccines became a 'key part of NHS plans'. Soon almost every child under the age of fifteen was vaccinated, leading to an immediate and dramatic reduction of both diseases.

Asthma and eczema were problematic for some children as medication was not very effective. Chicken pox and whooping cough were also prevalent, with long quarantine periods to reduce the spread of disease. One child who caught whooping cough remembers being off school for six months. On the doctor's advice, her mother took her daily on an open-top bus from Bournemouth to Shell Bay in Dorset, to spend the day on the beach in the fresh air.

In the early 1950s children in hospital were not allowed to see their parents except for an hour on Saturdays and Sundays, and they were often placed in adult wards. One boy recalled the trauma of being in hospital as a child: the anaesthetic rubber mask forced over his face, the sickness afterwards, with his parents not allowed to visit him. The experience gave him a negative view of hospitals that lasted all his life. Dr James Bowlby, later renowned for his research into child–parent bonding, helped make the 1952 documentary film *A Two Year Old Goes To Hospital*, to illustrate the 'impact of loss and suffering by a young child separated from his parents'. The film was instrumental in changing hospital restrictions, and from 1954 daily visits were slowly introduced.

By the late 1950s environmental dangers received greater attention. Post-war London children regularly endured acrid-smelling smog, caused by emissions from factories, power stations and innumerable coal fires hitting very cold air. The 'Great Smog' of 1952 began on 5 December. Without warning, after a bright cold start, an impenetrable fog formed, heralding five days of 'toxic darkness'. Transport ceased and 'theatres closed as smog invaded the auditoriums'. Sixty years later, on 5 December 2012, on BBC Radio 4's *Today* programme, Iris Young recalled her choking, frightening experience as the bus she was on hit a wall of smog, the road in front 'disappeared' and she found herself covered in grime and grit. Four thousand Londoners died in five days, with young children and the elderly

S.& W. Islington Schools' Swimming Association

Certificate

Awarded to John Shepherd

M. M. Latham.
Hon. Certificate Secretary.

September 26th 1951.

In affiliation with the London Schools Swimming Association.

A.Romey.

the most vulnerable. A positive outcome from the 1952 smog tragedy was the 1956 Clean Air Act, which created smokeless city zones, with initial grants to help people replace coal with cleaner electric or gas fires.

In the early 1950s smoking was rife – in cinemas, restaurants, shops and all public places. Many doctors smoked. Psychiatrists were known to offer their patients a cigarette to 'put them at their ease'. The journalist James Naughtie later recalled: 'Everywhere, smoke got in your eyes.' There was no law against children buying cigarettes; many parents sent their children to buy ten 'Senior Service' or cheaper 'Woodbines'. Children also bought 'sweet cigarettes', edible tubes that looked like the real cigarettes their parents smoked.

However, in 1954 Richard Doll's seminal report in the *British Medical Journal*, later confirmed in a 1962 report from the Royal College of Surgeons, established the association between smoking and lung cancer. Data from the 1958 National Child Development Study survey also revealed that mothers who smoked during pregnancy harmed their foetuses. Campaigners began in earnest to highlight the dangers. By 1965 tobacco advertising on television ceased, and the anti-smoking lobby grew from strength to strength.

Islington Schools Swimming Association awarded certificates to children in the borough. The old-fashioned swimming costumes portrayed suggest that older-style certificates were still in use in austerity Britain of the early 1950s.

SHOPPING

After school [in 1958], we would pop into the local sweetshop, crammed with rows of large glass jars full of different colourful sweets. I always bought a 2d chocolate bar or Sherbet Lemons. Sweets were weighed out, usually 2 ounces or a quarter of a pound, and put into paper bags that were folded over or twisted at the top to stop them falling out.

CHILDREN were delighted when sweets were de-rationed in 1953, at a time when rationing still dominated family life. To buy rationed articles, each person registered at a chosen shop and received a book of coupons, individually cancelled when a purchase was made. Shopkeepers were provided with only enough food for registered customers, leading to great competition. In 1952 two butchers vying for shoppers on Woodberry Down Council Estate in north London fought over a customer's ration book, rolling around in the sawdust still commonly used on the floors of butchers' shops. The 1984 black comedy *A Private Function* showed how hard it was to manage without resorting to the black market – the illegal buying and selling of goods – in the post-war austerity years. Shopping for food was a lengthy process as items had to be purchased from several different specialist shops, such as the grocer, the greengrocer, the butcher, the baker and the fishmonger.

At larger grocers, such as Sainsbury's, customers queued for different items at separate counters. Bacon was sliced to order, and a thin wire was pulled through huge blocks of cheese to divide it into small lumps. Butter was cut from a large slab and patted into shape with patterned wooden spatulas, leaving an imprint on the butter, sometimes a flower or leaf pattern. Eggs had a little 'red lion' stamp on each one to ensure quality: 'We had to check each egg was stamped; that meant it was good to eat,' Gill remembered. Grocers such as the Co-op or Lipton's would sell broken biscuits at a cheaper price, and they became a staple purchase for many households.

Opposite:
An advertisement for Spangles sweets, 1952. 'Neatly wrapped, neatly packed … and so refreshing', Spangles were a popular sweet in the 1950s but, like Punch Bars and 'gob-stoppers', they were later discontinued. Sweets that survived into the twenty-first century included Smarties and Mars bars.

In small village shops big open sacks sat on the floor, sometimes containing prunes, carrots or potatoes. Mary remembered shelves 'stacked with cleaning products like Vim and Ajax, Flash or Harpic. There were wooden clothes pegs that we girls loved to turn into puppets, next to tins of Spam or corned beef.'

There were also home deliveries. In the early 1950s milk was usually delivered in glass bottles, brought by horse and cart. In some rural areas milk still often arrived in a churn and was then ladled into the household's jugs. Other door-to-door deliveries included the travelling baker and the 'Corona pop man', who came 'on a Friday selling bottles of lemonade'. The empty bottles were always returned, as they were worth 2d each.

There was special dispensation for the Coronation and, in an otherwise austerity 1953 budget, each adult was allowed one extra pound of sugar and 4 ounces of margarine in order to bake celebratory cakes. The national festive mood was enhanced as shops decorated their premises in honour of the occasion.

Going to certain shops was a common experience for most children. Woolworth's at Christmas was a child's delight, with colourful baubles, crackers, and folded paper decorations that could be pulled out into streamers to stretch across a room. Julia remembers buying a medicine glass as a present for her mother, while another girl bought a bread bin, convinced her mother would be delighted.

One of the most fascinating childhood shopping experiences was visiting drapers' and department stores that used aerial cash systems, known as 'flying foxes' or 'rapid wire systems'. When a customer bought an item,

The well-known high-street stores F. W. Woolworth and Marks & Spencer were decorated with flags and bunting to celebrate the Queen's Coronation, Cambridge, 1953.

the assistant would take 'a large wooden ball, unscrew it, place the bill and money inside, screw it up again and put it in an upright chute. She either pulled something or worked a lever. The ball shot up the chute onto an overhead railway track along the shop's ceiling, travelling along it to a cashier perched at a small illuminated window.' The bill, stamped 'PAID', together with any change, was then sent back down to the assistant to give to the customer.

By the mid-1950s shopping changed as 'supermarkets' gradually appeared on the high street. Early supermarkets had trolleys little bigger than a hand basket, but the change in shopping style was irrevocable. A greater range of products began appearing, for example several types of pasta, where previously there had been only macaroni. Indian and Chinese food grew in popularity, with 'chicken chop-suey and chips' appearing on the menu of every Butlin's holiday camp by the end of the decade. To compete with the new supermarkets, other firms began to diversify. Milkmen employed by the major rival dairies United and Express now carried bread, butter, cheese and vegetables for home delivery, using modern motorised floats instead of horses. In 'The Large Cool Store' (1961), inspired by the Marks & Spencer store in Hull,

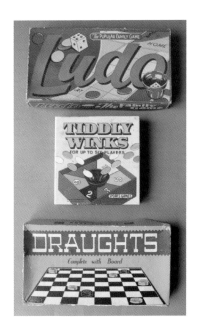

Three popular 1950s board games: Ludo, Tiddly Winks and Draughts.

The 'Land of Make Believe' jigsaw puzzle, dating from 1956. When two pieces were lost, cardboard replacements were made by a skilful father.

Queenie
Seeley's London
Co-operative
Society member's
pass book, 1954.
Her national
membership
earned her a
dividend, or share of
the Co-op's profits,
based on purchases.

The face of a
child sucking a
Rowntree's Fruit
Gum was a familiar
image in the 1950s.

the poet Philip Larkin marvelled at the far larger stock available in shops by the end of the decade:

The large cool store selling cheap clothes
Set out in simple sizes plainly …
heaps of trousers
Spread the stands

Toys gradually became more plentiful as the 1950s progressed. Cambridge's department store, Eaden Lilley, had a 'toy department in the basement with alluring displays of model railways, including the latest electric 00 gauge, plus Triang and Dinky cars in glass cases'. Toy shops also did a good trade in board games, including Monopoly and Snakes and Ladders. Jigsaw puzzles sold extremely well, particularly for young children. Dan Dare from the *Eagle* comic also appeared in jigsaws and annuals, boosting sales.

The greatest commercial success of the children's book world was Enid Blyton, at the height of her popularity in the 1950s. Each new book was eagerly awaited by millions of children. Her bestsellers were the 'Famous Five', 'Faraway Tree', 'Secret Seven', 'Adventure' and 'Mystery' series. Blyton's publishers also produced ephemera such as 'Famous Five' and 'Faraway Tree' card games.

By the second half of the decade a new affluence was beginning to be felt, even in historically poor northern towns such as Barnsley, Wigan and Stockton-on-Tees, where new estates promised materially better lives for the next generation. In 1956 the Ideal Home Exhibition exhibited its 'house of the future', full of colourful new designs, regarded as affordable by families with growing incomes.

Many 1950s' children remember reciting their parents' Co-operative dividend ('divvy') number off by heart to 'Co-op' shopkeepers. However, while stores such as Marks & Spencer modernised and thrived, 'Co-ops', based mainly in the industrial north or London and owned by customer shareholders, found it difficult to compete in the new, highly competitive environment that arose in the latter years of the decade.

By the late 1950s there was a surge in the number of households possessing a television set. The 1955 launch of commercial television promised a bright new world, targeting 'the family at home' with daily slogans and jingles advertising 'must have' products. 'Snap, crackle and pop', 'Go to work on an egg' and the first Oxo commercial with the idealised nuclear family were so memorable that they were selected as favourites by Channel 4 viewers nearly fifty years later. Advertisers soon began to focus on children as a separate consumer group, most notably with advertisements for sweets and cereals.

By the later 1950s the concept of teenagers as a separate group with money to spend took hold. Magazines such as 'romantic' *Valentine* (1957) and *Roxy* (1958), with its 'Alma Cogan Glamour School', specifically targeted teenage girls. The 'goal', according to a *Valentine* quiz, was marriage: 'Will you be an ideal wife? If your husband asked you, would you give up your job?' The correct answer was 'yes'. Even *Girl*, with its schoolgirl readership, began to highlight the importance of appearance by the late 1950s. 'Someone is always looking at you … Your beauty can never take time off,' urged an advertisement for Boots No. 7 cosmetics.

From 1954 teenagers flocked to the new Wimpy Bars serving American-style hamburgers. The following year, Mary Quant opened her shop Bazaar in King's Road, Chelsea, and by 1958 Carnaby Street was open for business, providing 'super trendy but inexpensive' clothes, later becoming London's 'leading fashion epicentre' for the younger generation. There were also opportunities for teenagers to earn money and gain some independence, by helping the milkman, doing paper rounds or obtaining Saturday jobs. Quite a few teenagers worked in Woolworth's for '10s 6d a day, an insurance stamp and the very early lunch break that no-one else wanted'.

'You've never had it so good!' ran a 1959 Conservative Party advertisement, echoing Harold Macmillan's earlier statement, as the Tories won their third consecutive general election.

This 1957 advertisement for the high-sugar, honey-flavoured wheat cereal Sugar Puffs was specifically aimed at children and included a free toy.

Two children stare in the window of the kiosk of Boots the chemist at Waterloo station, 1955. By this time Boots offered photographic developing as well as pharmaceutical products, toiletries and cosmetics.

41

RECREATION AND ENTERTAINMENT

We come along on Saturday morning,
Greeting everybody with a smile.
We come along on Saturday morning,
Knowing that it's all worthwhile!
(Sung with gusto at Saturday morning pictures, Dalston Odeon)

FOR MANY the new decade did not really begin until May 1951 and the launch of the hugely successful Festival of Britain. Seen as a post-war 'tonic', the Festival looked to the future, celebrating modern British architecture and industrial achievements. The ambitious Royal Festival Hall, designed by Sir Hugh Casson and still standing in 2013, arose on London's South Bank, surrounded by restaurants and public spaces. The Lansbury Estate in Poplar, still also existing in 2013 under the shadow of Canary Wharf, was part of the Festival's 'living architecture' legacy.

Children in the 1950s were fascinated by the science exhibits, such as doors with sensors that opened 'as if by magic'. Bernice, who travelled up from Kent, remembered passing bombed-out houses before having her photograph taken next to the iconic cigar-shaped Skylon steel tower that dominated the Festival complex. The Skylon and the nearby Dome of Discovery, then the largest dome in the world, became the instantly recognisable symbols of the exhibition.

As part of the Festival, Battersea Park was transformed into Battersea Pleasure Gardens, with a new water garden, fountains, a 'Tree Walk', and the famous Battersea Fun Fair, with its spectacular ride, a wooden-constructed rollercoaster named 'The Big Dipper'.

Two years later, on 2 June 1953, the coronation of Queen Elizabeth II heralded a 'new Elizabethan age'. For the first time the British public felt part of an historic occasion, as television brought the ceremony into many living rooms, mainly through flickering 9-inch black-and-white sets. Others peered at televisions in shop windows or went to their neighbours to watch. One guest, the Queen of Tonga, was acclaimed as she rode in an open

Opposite:
Children feeding
the pigeons in
Trafalgar Square
on a day out in
London.

43

Two official postcards of the South Bank at the Festival of Britain. The Royal Festival Hall, seen in in the lower image, was still functioning in 2013.

A map of the South Bank Exhibition area for the Festival of Britain, 1951, shows the new Royal Festival Hall, the large Dome of Discovery, and the numerous pavilions, restaurants and walkways.

carriage through rain-swept London. Huge street parties were held across the land. Allan remembered his father making red, white and blue crepe flowers to go 'around each gateway' for a Welsh street party. The daily lives of the royal family assumed a new importance, featuring in women's and girls' magazines. Readers of *Girl* read that Princess Anne 'mostly wears plaid skirts or even corduroy trousers, the same clothes worn by children all over Britain'.

Girl also projected the upper-middle-class world of 'ballerinas and horse-riding'. 'Belle of the Ballet' became one of *Girl*'s longest-running serials, as across the country young girls were inspired to attend ballet lessons and to learn how to dance like the Royal Ballet's most famous

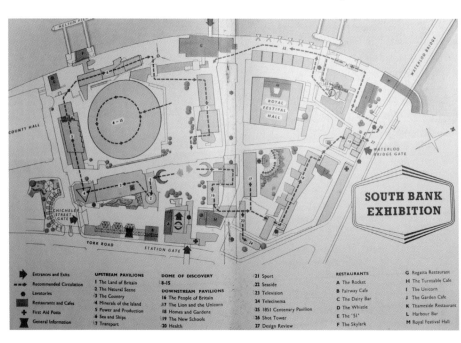

classical dancer, Margot Fonteyn. Schoolgirl Jennifer Gay, who, aged fourteen, became the first children's television presenter, left the BBC in 1953 to train as a ballerina.

For many children the only place to be on Saturday in the 1950s was the cinema. In 1955 nearly two thousand venues screened children's matinées, 'Saturday Morning Pictures'. At the Bournemouth Odeon, 6d 'took you in, but 9d took you upstairs'. The noise was deafening. Children cheered the cartoons, cowboys and comedians, and joined in well-known songs. Weekly serials, strongly influenced by the United States, included *Hopalong Cassidy*, *The Lone Ranger*, *Superman*, *Lassie* or *Tarzan*, starring Johnny Weismuller. Many low-budget black-and-white Saturday 'healthy adventure' films were made by the Children's Film Foundation (CFF), in which 'brave resourceful children' were commended by the police as a 'credit to the nation'. The first adaptation of Enid Blyton's *Five on a Treasure Island* appeared as an eight-week CFF serial in 1957. Pathé News was also shown, introduced by a crowing cockerel, and everyone stood up

Janet Seeley plays a fairy in a 1950s' Christmas ballet show.

A Festival of Britain children's fancy-dress competition, with the Mayor of Poplar; Battersea Park, 17 October 1951.

for the National Anthem at the end of the performance. School trips to the cinema were rare, although some classes saw *The Conquest of Everest*, a documentary celebrating the first ascent of the mountain, by Edmund Hillary and Sherpa Tenzing in 1953, the news of which was announced to the nation on Coronation Day.

Cinema audiences remained high. Many baby-boomers remember being taken to see *Treasure Island*, and also *Davy Crockett, King of the Wild Frontier*, whose escapades were re-enacted in many school playgrounds. Young and old enjoyed the Ealing comedies, such as *The Lavender Hill Mob* (1951) and *The Ladykillers* (1955).

Dreams, excitement and escapism – Saturday morning at the pictures.

Teenagers were enamoured by the glamour of Hollywood, particularly with musicals such as *Carousel* and *Oklahoma*, and 'blockbusters' such as *The Ten Commandments* (1956) and *Ben Hur* (1959), while *Monsieur Hulot's Holiday*, 'a silent French wordless 1953 classic' comedy, entertained a minority. One of the first films shown at the newly opened ABC cinema in Golders Green in 1956 was *War and Peace*, which was so long it included the unprecedented feature of an intermission. *The Wizard of Oz* began in black and white, and then 'Dorothy opened the door to let in a burst of colour'; for Raymond, who saw it in Norwich, it remained forever his favourite film.

Children were encouraged to be 'out and about' in the 1950s. One popular activity was 'train-spotting'. Using the *ABC Guide to Locomotives*, passionate young spotters noted all the engines they saw. Jean and her

Thurston and Sons' roundabout and amusements at the annual Midsummer Fair, Cambridge, c. 1950s.

brother, Jim, were allowed 'beside the driver as he worked the engine... Jim became such good friends with the station master that he was given his old uniform cap.' In the early 1950s millions travelled by train but by mid-decade, with the increase in car ownership and the start of Britain's motorway system, rail began to be challenged by road.

Fairs and circuses were in their heyday in the early to mid-1950s, with Bertram Mills's, Chipperfield's and Billy Smart's troupes travelling across Britain, providing magical escapism, 'as close as most people got to the glamour of Hollywood'. Dazzling high-wire aerial acts and cages with dangerous wild animals, later also seen on television, brought thrills and excitement, relieving the tedium of daily lives.

Family days out increased as austerity lessened. In the days before foreign travel became the norm, trips to local seaside resorts were frequently by coach; northerners often headed for Blackpool, southerners to Brighton or Clacton-on-Sea.

Butlin's and Pontin's holiday camps provided communal holidays, with everyone eating together and listening for the frequent loudspeaker announcements. Children enjoyed making sandcastles with metal buckets and sharp spades, and eating the favourite post-war treat, ice-cream.

Local events were of great significance, especially in rural areas, as many children did not travel away from their home districts. London's children,

A 1953 advertisement for Butlin's holiday camps, 'the best of all family holidays'. *Inset*: the Watson family, nearest the camera, enjoy a communal meal at Butlin's, *c.* 1958.

47

far from the sea, rode on trams and trolley-buses to visit the capital's museums and famous sites such as the Tower of London, Madame Tussaud's waxworks and the adjacent London Planetarium. Opened in 1958, the Planetarium seated over three hundred people looking skywards into the huge horizontal dome to watch shows about space and astronomy.

Zoos had a boost after Brumas, the first polar bear to be successfully reared in captivity, was born in London Zoo in November 1949. Mistakenly thought by many to be male, she became a major celebrity, even lending her name to a song: 'B-R-U-M-A-S, B-R-U-M-A-S, B-R-U-M-A-S spells BRUMAS!' Her arrival led to record attendance figures for London Zoo in 1950.

Many children, especially those with few books at home, belonged to libraries.

Villages still traditionally made their own entertainment. A young girl is crowned Queen of the May in Meldreth, Cambridgeshire, in 1958.

Private subscription libraries, as run by Boots the chemist, still existed alongside free libraries. However, when John took his pre-school age brother Robert to join the new public library in Stoke Newington, Robert was refused a ticket because 'he could not yet read'.

Home entertainment was dominated by BBC Radio. Family comedy programmes enjoyed by the whole family included *Take It from Here*, *Educating Archie* and the inimitable *Goon Show*. *Children's Hour*, from 5 to 6 p.m. each weekday evening, broadcast popular serials such as *Jennings at School* and the adventures of the boy detectives Norman and Henry Bones. Its best-known programme, *Toytown*, featured Larry the Lamb, played by 'every child's favourite broadcaster', Derek McCulloch, better known as 'Uncle Mac'. *Listen with Mother* was a fifteen-minute programme for pre-school children that ran from 1950 to 1982. It always began with the words, 'Are you sitting comfortably? Then I'll begin.'

Brumas, the polar bear, born at London Zoo in Regent's Park, attracted huge crowds throughout the 1950s until her death in 1959.

On Saturday mornings 'Uncle Mac' presented *Children's Favourites*, a musical request programme avidly followed by millions of children. They heard Max Bygraves's 'I'm a Pink Toothbrush, You're a Blue Toothbrush' and American hits such as 'I Taut I Taw a Puddy Tat' and Danny Kaye's 'Little White Duck'. In 1953 Lita Roza topped the British charts with her version of the American song, 'How Much Is That Doggie in the Window?'

Stories broadcast on children's radio programmes in the 1950s were sometimes published in book form: *Uncle Mac's Children's Hour Book* and *Listen with Mother* 's 'favourite stories for little ones'.

By 1950 the early evening serial *Dick Barton*, with its dramatic theme tune, 'The Devil's Gallop', was a 'pop cultural landmark before the term existed'. Although not intended for children, it soon became clear that millions of youngsters tuned into the Light Programme at 6.45 each evening to hear 'Dick and his mates solve crime and save the nation from disaster'. The programme ended in 1951, because it was said to have a bad influence on the young. In 2006, 338 lost episodes (of an original 712) were found in Australia, sixty years after the first broadcast.

Many of the young listeners who mourned the demise of *Dick Barton* turned two years later to *Journey into Space* (1953–8), a half-hour BBC Radio

Children borrowing library books at East Ham library, c. 1950.

science fiction programme that always ended with a dramatic cliff-hanger. It was set in 1965, when its writer, BBC producer Charles Chilton, thought men would first walk on the moon. Despite its scientific inaccuracies, it became the last British radio programme to attract a larger evening audience than television. Well-known cast members were David Kossoff, Alfie Bass, Deryck Guyler and David Jacobs, who played twenty-two different characters. The programme's young fans included the future scientist Stephen Hawking, comedian Kenny Everett and Prime Minister John Major.

Whole families also listened to *The Archers*, an 'everyday story of country folk', which replaced *Dick Barton*'s early evening slot from 1951. The episode of 22 September 1955 was possibly the most memorable, with the death of Grace Archer in a fire at Brookfield Farm. The BBC switchboard was jammed by calls from distraught listeners. Intentionally or not, the broadcast was timed to coincide with the launch of Britain's first commercial television station. In 2013 *The Archers* remained the world's longest running 'soap opera'.

A family gathers round the television for an evening's entertainment, c. 1957.

Although few homes had television until after the Coronation, BBC TV was already catering for children and growing families. Annette Mills (sister of the actor John Mills) starred with *Muffin the Mule* from 1946 to 1955, and *Children's Newsreel* ran throughout the decade. Hugely successful *Whirligig* began in 1950, *Andy Pandy* in 1952. *The Appleyards*, with their four children, and *The Groves Family* saga (1954–7) attracted a large family audience. From 1955 Independent Television reached millions of viewers of all ages; an early success, *The Adventures of Robin Hood*, starring Richard Greene, ran weekly until 1959.

Although BBC Radio provided some popular music, by the mid-1950s many teenagers tuned to a new commercial station, Radio Luxembourg, for greater coverage of up-to-date pop music from American stars such as Louis Armstrong, Nat 'King' Cole and Bing Crosby. The 1956 American film *Blackboard Jungle*, featuring rock and roll music by Bill Hayley, resulted in cinema riots by teddy boys when it was first shown in Britain. There were far fewer British pop stars, but Billy Fury, Marty Wilde and Tommy Steele all emerged before the end of the decade. Jiving was the latest craze, and in 1959 Cliff Richard, with his backing group the Shadows, achieved his first number one hit with 'Livin' Doll'.

A *Dick Barton Special Agent* book, published in 1950 to complement the radio programme, included nine stories featuring Dick and his 'sidekicks', Snowy and Jock.

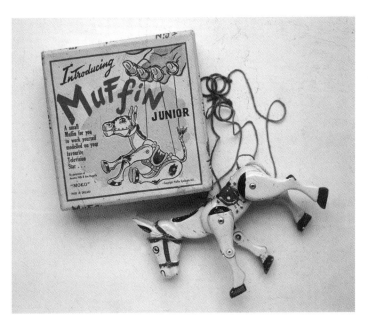

The 'Muffin the Mule' puppet, linked to the television programme of the same name, sold well.

Members of the
Green Rose Cycling
Club from Plaistow
in east London take
a break at Ramsden
Heath, Essex, while
on a ride to Maldon,
July 1958.

Sport played an important part in many children's lives. Cricket, netball, hockey and football were all played at school. Junior football expanded, with boys playing for numerous small football clubs in local amateur leagues. Cycling attracted many youngsters who joined cycling clubs across the country.

Roller-skating became a craze for both boys and girls, and in London Alexandra Palace and Victoria Park, Hackney, attracted thousands of young skaters. Even younger children, not allowed on the rinks, would skate with varying degrees of skill along pavements.

From the mid-1950s young enthusiasts watched live television coverage of England's cricket test matches against Australia and tennis from Wimbledon.

Children at
the open-air
roller-skating rink
in Victoria Park,
Hackney, London,
1954.

Denis Compton, Peter May, Fred Trueman, Maria Bueno and Lew Hoad became household names. Yet few football matches appeared live on television, except for Wembley Cup Finals, notably the 1953 'Stanley Matthews final' in which Blackpool defeated Bolton Wanderers

Football practice and matches for schoolboys were often arranged during school holidays. The footballer Walley Barnes gives advice to young members of the Football Association's Colts XI at half-time during a match at the Oval, c. 1958.

4-3. Instead, boys joined their fathers on the terraces on Saturday afternoons to cheer on their local team. The Munich Air Disaster on 6 February 1958, in which eight of Manchester United's young team, the 'Busby Babes', were among the twenty-three fatalities, was the most tragic event in post-war British football.

By 1959 life in Britain had changed from the post-war world of 1950. Growing economic prosperity had given families more disposable income, and most had a better standard of living than ever before, with more time to spend on leisure pursuits. By the close of the decade, the dominant medium of choice for recreation and entertainment was television, leading to a more sedentary lifestyle for many families.

The victorious Arsenal team arrive in an open-top bus for a municipal reception after defeating Liverpool 2-0 in the 1950 FA Cup Final. Many children were in the crowd outside Islington Town Hall.

FURTHER READING

Beckett, Francis. *What Did the Baby Boomers Ever Do For Us?* Biteback, 2010.

Chetwynd, Harriet. *Comprehensive School: The Story of Woodberry Down.* Routledge & Kegan Paul, 1960.

Cooke, David. *Dinky Toys.* Shire, 2005.

Cooke, David. *Corgi Toys.* Shire, 2008.

Feeney, Paul. *A 1950s Childhood: From Tin Baths to Bread and Dripping.* The History Press, 2009.

Ferry, Kathryn. *The 1950s Kitchen.* Shire, 2011.

Good Housekeeping: *The Best of the 1950s.* Collins & Brown, 2008.

Haverson, Neil (editor). *Let's Talk: Schooldays* (in Norfolk). Jarrold, 2005.

Hennessey, Peter. *Having It So Good: Britain in the 1950s.* Allen Lane, 2006.

Kynaston, David. *Family Britain 1951–57.* Bloomsbury, 2010.

Leighton, Sophie. *The 1950s Home.* Shire, 2011.

Opie, Robert. *The 1950s Scrapbook.* New Cavendish Books, 1998.

Opie, Robert. *Remember When: A Nostalgic Trip through the Consumer Era.* Bounty Books, 2006.

Tatarsky, Daniel (editor). *Eagle Annual: The Best of the 1950s Comic.* Orion Books, 2007.

Woodberry Down Memories Group. *Woodberry Down Memories: The History of an LCC Housing Estate.* ILEA, 1989.

Worth, Jennifer. *Call the Midwife: A True Story of the East End in the 1950s.* Phoenix, 2012.

Young, Michael, and Willmott, Peter. *Family and Kinship in East London.* Penguin Books, 1980.

PLACES TO VISIT

Basildon Park, Lower Basildon, Reading RG8 9NR.
   Telephone: 0118 984 3040.
   Website: www.nationaltrust.org.uk/basildon-park (1950s' kitchen.)
Bethnal Green Museum of Childhood, Cambridge Heath Road, London
   E2 9PA. Telephone: 020 8983 5200.
   Website: www.museumofchildhood.org.uk
Brighton Toy and Model Museum, 52–55 Trafalgar Street, Brighton
   BN1 4EB. Telephone: 01273 749494.
   Website: www.brightontoymuseum.co.uk
Coventry Toy Museum, Whitefriars Gate, Much Park Street,
   Coventry CV1 2LT. Telephone: 024 7622 7560.
   Website: www.coventrytoymuseum75501.coventry.towntalk.co.uk
Geffrye Museum, Kingsland Road, London E2 8EA.
   Telephone: 020 7739 9893. Website: www.geffrye-museum.org.uk
Kettle's Yard, Castle Street, Cambridge CB3 0AQ.
   Telephone: 01223 748100. Website: www.kettlesyard.co.uk
Museum of Childhood Memories, 1 Castle Street, Beaumaris, Anglesey
   LL58 8AP. Telephone: 01248 712498.
   Website: www.nwi.co.uk/museumofchildhood
Museum of the 50s Era, Cae Dai Trust, Denbigh, North Wales LL16 4SU.
   Telephone: 01745 817004. Website: www.hiraethog.org.uk
Newarke Houses and Gardens, The Newarke, Leicester LE2 7BY.
   Telephone: 0116 225 4980. Website: www.museum@leicester.gov.uk
   (1950s' street scene.)
Romney, Hythe and Dymchurch Toy and Model Museum, New Romney Station,
   New Romney, Kent TN28 8PL. Telephone: 01797 362353.
   Website: www.rhdr.org.uk/pages/toy.html
Victoria and Albert Museum, Cromwell Road, London SW7 2RL.
   Telephone: 020 7942 2000. Website: www.vam.ac.uk

INDEX